CONFLICT RESOLUTION FOR A PEACEFUL WORLD

"We are all the leaves of one tree.
We are all the waves of one ocean."

Thich Nhat Hanh

COPYRIGHT NOTICE

WARNING!

Most people will not want to hear the simple, underlying truth about conflict this short book offers. It will provoke a strong reaction in some because it is disruptive to how we all behave now and have done so for millennia! We have become a destructive species, of ourselves and our environment, having developed our intellect to become very clever but at the expense of becoming wise.

Almost everyone, when asked, will say they want to live in a peaceful world but only a few are prepared to do what it takes to have such a world. Most prefer the drama of their lives with all its highs and lows, wanting the world to change whilst they stay the same.

Cause and effect are inseparable.

DEDICATION

A debt of gratitude is owed to my family, friends and everyone I have met, in person or online, all of whom have been my teachers through this journey we call Life. In particular, thanks go to James Waite and Brian Thompson for reading through the manuscript, checking for errors and commenting on its content. I should also mention Judi Rhodes who during the 1990's, created and moderated "The End of the Rope Ranch" group on the Internet. Her uncompromising approach revealed my immaturity, shattered my illusions and battered my ego into submission. Thank you Judi!

AUTHOR BACKGROUND

Several years as a community mediator(1), working under the title "Conflict to Consensus". Operated within a regional community, which included both urban and rural areas. Previously worked in the defence sector and before that a student of International Relations. There was an underlying interest in understanding why conflicts arise, how we attempt to resolve them and why those attempts, even if they appear successful initially, can fail later on.

The author is not important. **YOU**, the reader, are important. Ultimately, this book is about you!

You will interpret and assess its contents in terms of your own past experience. However, you are being asked to **suspend judgement** until you have reached the end of the book. It is short and simple!

A NOTE ABOUT SEMANTICS

All words are defined in terms of other words and sometimes different meanings are ascribed to the same word. In this book the word 'consciousness' is used to mean exactly the same as 'awareness', 'presence', 'knowing' and 'being'. This is because some of the quotes mentioned use the word 'consciousness' as it has been employed historically.

CONTENTS

INTRODUCTION 1

CONFLICT IS HAPPENING RIGHT NOW! 2

CONFLICT RESOLUTION TODAY 4

ONE ROOT CAUSE OF ALL
HUMAN CONFLICT 10

A CLOSER LOOK: WHAT IS THE MIND? 14

THE MYTH OF THE SEPARATE SELF 19

HOW THE EGOIC MIND
CREATES CONFLICT 22

THOUGHT IS THE PROBLEM 28

IN PURSUIT OF PEACE 30

CAN WE CHOOSE TO EVOLVE? 33

THE ELEMENTS OF DIALOGUE 36

THE CONFLICT RESOLVER'S ROLE 40

IS THERE ANYTHING MORE? 47

NOTES 50

FURTHER READING 53

INTRODUCTION

Much of humanity's recorded history has been about conflict. It was and remains inevitable because we are unaware of how we are creating it.

This is not another 'how to' book. It is not about mediation processes, or how to get past 'no' to 'yes'. There are no clever methods to overcome blockages, 'win' negotiations or achieve 'win-win' outcomes. Books that do this enable existing circumstances to continue. They do not bring about a fundamental resolution of conflict at its root.

This book points to the root cause of all human conflict and what we must do to end it.

It is not a book for intellectuals. It is a book for everyone and is written to be easily comprehensible. If you are interested in conflict and its resolution, both within and beyond yourself, then it is a book for you. At the end you will be left with work to do on yourself.

All any of us have to do in fact is see what is right in front of us.

We never look!

CONFLICT IS HAPPENING RIGHT NOW!

*"How much energy they put into harming each other.
How little into saving."*

Suzanne Collins

At the time of writing, at all levels, right now, there are many conflicts occurring in the world. It is nothing new.

The most serious involves Russia and Ukraine. With Ukraine having support from NATO member countries the conflict has the potential to become a nuclear confrontation.

Not far behind it in terms of seriousness is China's threat to invade Taiwan which it sees as a rogue Chinese state, whilst Taiwan insists it is a sovereign, independent state.

It is not just countries that are in conflict with one another. There are other major conflicts, involving civil or drug wars and/or terrorist insurgency in Yemen, Palestine, Ethiopia, Haiti, Myanmar, Mexico, Somalia, Libya, the Central African Republic, Syria, Afghanistan, and the Democratic Republic of Congo.

Beyond these conflicts there are innumerable lesser ones occurring. Religious and ethnic groups are in conflict with one another, neighbours are in conflict with one another, family members are in conflict with one another, and even children are sometimes in conflict with one another.

It looks like a complex situation but the root cause of all human conflict is simple. It is a consequence of the existing human predicament which makes conflict inevitable in everyone's life at some point. When has there not been some type of conflict somewhere on planet Earth? From ancient tribal disputes, through the two 'world wars' up to today, conflict is mainly responsible for the system of apparently separate nation states we now live in.

The war between Russia and Ukraine, with the latter being supported by NATO countries, has highlighted the fact that Russia's relationship with NATO has always been fractious. When Mr. Putin came to power in the year 2000, the possibility of Russia joining NATO was raised. At a meeting between Russian and NATO delegates President Putin asked the question, "When are you going to invite Russia to join NATO?". The response was you don't get an invite, you have to apply to join NATO.

That posturing exchange summed up the human dilemma. From children arguing over toys, through family and neighbour disputes, to international conflicts, it is the very same thing going on.

Unbelievable? Read on.

CONFLICT RESOLUTION TODAY

There is nothing new in this short and simple book. Its content however may be new to practising conflict resolvers(2) as well as those interested in the subject area.

The root cause of all human conflict is not to be found in any standard conflict resolution book. Such books never address fundamentals but instead outline standardised methodologies for resolving conflicts.

There is no standardised methodology for resolving any and all conflicts. People and situations are unique. Consequently what is required is an appropriate contextual response.

Conflict resolvers who believe their particular methodology will solve any and all conflicts are fooling themselves. They are approaching every conflict wearing a mental 'straight jacket'! One day a set of circumstances will arise and their particular methodology will fail.

Standardised conflict resolution methodologies are based on research and testing. The assumption is that acquiring knowledge about conflicts will enable us to resolve all of them. It will not! It cannot! Knowledge is always bounded by ignorance. We know our concepts but not the actuality of things. Whilst we can have empathy with others, we cannot be them, think the same thoughts, or experience things as they do.

Everyone is unique.

Every situation is unique.

Begin with this fact and always look at the entire context of a situation.

People become conflict resolvers for different reasons. Some truly hate conflict and want to help people resolve their interpersonal issues. For others it is an ego desire to be seen to be doing good or be a good person. Yet others have fallen into it as part of their job, maybe as a solicitor or lawyer.

Seeking to understand human conflict can take us into studying sociology, politics, science, psychology, religion and spirituality. If you are going down that route **STOP!** The answer is not 'out there'. Self knowledge is the way to go!

You say you know me,
You know me not.
You do not know your self,
So how can you know me?
First know your self,
Then you will know me… and everyone else too!

(WHAT! See the explanation that follows.)

Know Thyself

The Greek writer Pausanias stated that 'Know Thyself' was the first of three maxims inscribed in the forecourt of the Temple of Apollo at Delphi. This maxim is the most important message ever given to humanity.

Conflict resolution training involves 'self reflection', the same as many counselling training approaches. However that 'me', that 'self' is taken for granted.

This is **THE** fundamental error.

The thing we know the least about is our self! We are born ignorant, are conditioned by the society and culture we are born into, accept most if not everything we are told throughout our lifetime and die ignorant of who and what we are in reality.

Know your self intimately first, then you will have a better understanding of the participants involved in any conflict. The simple truth is that at our depth we are One!

Our consciousness is not ours but the consciousness of humanity.

This is a fundamental understanding. Ultimately we are all the same, regardless of our sex, race, nationality, or our religion. Everyone of us laughs, everyone of us cries; the same consciousness.

A question to contemplate: If I were you and you were me, what conflict between us could there be? What is your answer?

....

Still thinking about it?

Standing on the seashore,
Looking out to sea.
I see a wave arising,
And name it after me.

From an uncertain beginning,
To a crescendo rising high.
Suddenly I see the beach approaching,
And fear I am going to die.

Crashing on the seashore,
There is nothing more to see.
A final thought arises,
"Is this the end of me?".

Slipping from the seashore,
Into the vastness of the sea.
There is no separation,
The sea was always me!

Meaning: Each of us is a 'wave' on an ocean of life. Waves (people) appear to be separate from each other but they are never separate from the ocean (of life) itself. We are life! Life is us!

Waves on the surface of an ocean may look different but, no matter how varied the waves, at its depths an ocean is still and silent. As 'waves' on an ocean of life we are the same.

The difference between us and ocean waves is thought; we think! We think most of the time except when we are absorbed in something, 'knocked out', or in deep, dreamless sleep. Then our minds are totally still, silent.

We never really look at ourselves being almost completely focused on our external world. We do not want to see, afraid of what we might find or, perhaps lose.

(You didn't really have to think about the above question did you? The answer is obvious.)

ONE ROOT CAUSE OF ALL HUMAN CONFLICT

There are many different types of conflict with each of them having varied causes. Underlying all of them is a singular root cause of ALL human conflict.

It is so simple that the complicated human mind cannot see it. Nor does it want to! When the human mind hears what that underlying cause is it reacts, often with incredulity, sometimes with angry denial and possibly violently. That objection is always the same:

"IT'S NOT THAT SIMPLE!"

Yes, it is!

The human mind responding as it does is indicative of what the fundamental root cause is:

THE HUMAN MIND ITSELF!

It is the discriminatory, self-protective mechanism in our life which unknowingly defines and creates our problems. From minor irritations through to severe threats, the way the mind functions means conflict is inevitable.

This ultimate cause guides our actions as we move through our days and even in our dreams. It disappears completely in deep, dreamless sleep but its capacity to act remains.

Can you feel a resistance, small or large, maybe even anger arising in you as you read this? Then you have already proven to yourself what has been stated above.

We can sum up the root cause of all human conflict, by simply choosing to use a single word: IGNORANCE (of who and what we really are), or BELIEF (in being a separate self, our core belief), or quite simply SEPARATION.

We are ignorant of who and what we really are because we never look. Our focus is on our external world whilst taking our inner world for granted. Belief implies doubt. Whether they be cultural, religious, or even scientific, beliefs are 'sticking plasters' (band aids) to cover over what we do not know – and therefore usually fear. They serve to cover up our ignorance.

Separation is the belief that we are separate from everyone and everything else; an individual entity. You the reader think this, don't you? Look again. It doesn't take much effort to see that everyone and everything exists in relationship to everyone and everything else.

We think of ourselves as these physical bodies alone, yet they depend on air, food, water and sunshine to stay alive. The body itself is composed of many organs and is made from trillions of cells. Where does the 'self' begin and end?

People exist only in relationship to one another. Countries, which throughout history have come into being and then disappeared or had continually changing borders, exist only in relationship to one another.

All forms of physical matter exist only in relationship to other forms of physical matter. No thing has an independent existence. No thing exists outside of relationship!

> *"...there is no such thing as being isolated.*
> *to be, is to be related and without*
> *relationship there is no existence."*

Jiddu Krishnamurti(3)

The above quote is true, yet we still think and feel ourselves to be a separate, isolated individual, existing at the centre of our own particular universe. Nothing could be further from the truth but we will defend that lie with our life if necessary. Consequently conflict between people through to wars between nations is inevitable.

> *"All the activities that we know of as war are dominated or*
> *come from one single thought, "I am a separate self". That's*
> *it. That is the origin of all war and conflict…. Until the*
> *problem of conflict and war is dealt with at that level, in*
> *other words at its core, its root issue, conflict will continue."*

Rupert Spira(4)

THE ROOT CAUSE OF ALL HUMAN
CONFLICT IS THE CONDITIONED,
CONCEPTUALISING HUMAN MIND
WHICH DIVIDES, FRAGMENTS AND
SEPARATES EACH OF US FROM
EVERYONE AND EVERYTHING ELSE.

A CLOSER LOOK: WHAT IS THE MIND?

"There is something wrong with the way we think and as long as that is there everything we do will be a mess."

Alan Watts

There is no physical thing we call the mind. 'Mind' is a term for describing the process of thinking, one thought following another, to create a network of thought. Thoughts arise from the silent background of continuous consciousness. It is a hugely successful self defence mechanism which enables us to meet threats and survive. It has done so for millennia and in the process has enabled us to dominate every other species whilst also exploiting the planet's resources to our advantage.

The mind constitutes one thought process but it has two ways of thinking. The first is functional thought, which is concerned with physical survival, getting from A to B, finding food, etc. This is not a problem as it gets us through each day reasonably effectively. We take this form of thinking for granted and rarely notice it. The second is psychological thinking. This is the dominant form of thought that we are always aware of and think of as being 'normal'. Psychological thinking creates our sense of self, the 'ego', the 'I', we think ourselves to be. It pursues psychological survival and enhancement, leading us wanting to be a 'somebody' rather than a 'nobody'. It is this form of thinking that has led to the separation and consequent conflicts we experience today.

We are deceived into believing we are separate selves (ego's) because thought arises within particular bodies. Embodiment is the ego's covert advantage in surviving. We take it for granted and so are unaware of it. When the 'self' arises so does the 'other' and from that point on we are always subconsciously on guard, self protective and looking out for any threats, large or small. Watch your own mind for a moment

. . . .

Thoughts continually arise from the background consciousness without you having to deliberately think them. They have an effect in the body and then disappear back into that consciousness. We are not in control of them unless we try to deliberately think them. Mostly, they are in control of us.

Thought has created religion, culture, science and technology. The latter has enabled us to go to the moon, cure diseases, given us TV, smart phones, and the Internet so that we can communicate with people around the world whilst ignoring the person sitting next to us. It has also given us weapons of mutilation and mass destruction.

What would the world be like if thought identified with the community, the society or even the planet rather than the individual human? Would there be any conflict at all?

Most scientists are not aware of this!

Thought created the scientific method and thought protects that established orthodoxy. Why? Because the human mind wants continuity. It needs certainty and security to function efficiently.

Quantum Physics, at the forefront of scientific investigation, has had to come to terms with 'quantum inseparability'. That is, at the sub-atomic level no separate 'things' exist. Everything is connected to everything else in ways we have yet to fully understand. It appears that the entire universe is ultimately energy manifesting as everything that our senses experience. That includes you and me!

The problems for science do not stop there. The 'hard' problem for science is understanding the nature of consciousness which has no discernible and therefore measurable qualities. Many scientists claim that consciousness results from how the brain functions with the latest theory being vibrations in brain 'microtubuless'.

It is not in the interest of scientists to say "we do not know". They seek to maintain the validity and integrity of the discipline in order to sustain a sense of certainty and authority.

"Science cannot solve the ultimate mystery of nature. And that is because, in the last analysis, we ourselves are part of nature and therefore part of the mystery we are trying to solve."

Max Plank(5)

Science will remain incomplete until scientists have full knowledge of themselves. They are not separate from the experiments they conduct. They claim objectivity but they are in fact the subject in what for everyone is unavoidably a subject-object universe.

Always Moving, Never Still!

If everything were simple the human mind would not exist as it presently does. It has evolved through asking questions, thereby creating problems and then looking for answers. In finding answers it then generates more questions to find answers to. Have you ever wondered why some problems, including conflicts, have become so complex they now seem unsolvable?

Our busy lives are so 'mind captivating' that we never stop and look at what is actually happening, at why things are as they are; at why we live in fear, at why there is so little care and compassion in the world, at why conflict and wars are inevitable. It is a fact that the only separation we can find is in our conditioned minds. The crises we face are not 'out there'. They are a product of human (psychological) thinking.

THE MYTH OF THE SEPARATE SELF

"Is then the collapse of the idea of 'me'
our natural or normal state?"

Steven Harrison

The arising of the separative ego is not our fault but it is our responsibility. We are born into pre-existing societal and cultural circumstances. Our experiences within them condition the mind through experiencing; family, education, religion, society, media, in fact everything. We are our experiences!

We can ask ourselves simple questions:

What did I do to get my life?

Am I this body? (Following this, If I lose a part or parts of this body do I still exist?)

Am I my mind? If so, when thought ends do I also end?

If I am not my sense of self, ego, then who or what am I?

In noticing the noise of thought we ignore entirely the background silence of consciousness, even though that consciousness is the foundation for all thought. Thought needs consciousness to exist. Consciousness does not need thought to exist. Look for yourself!

Adyashanti(6)

To repeat, nothing exists outside of relationship. To prove this all we need to do is focus our attention and look for a centre within the body or mind which is uniquely and identifiably 'I'.(7)

Simply close your eyes and look for that centre within the body and mind. Concentrate intensely on this task. Do it for a few minutes.

. . . .

If you find that centre, then where are you looking at it from? Now find that and continue repeating the process until it becomes apparent.

. . . .

IT IS NOT THERE!

(If you disagree, then you are witnessing the self-protective mind in action.)

In focusing our attention we bring the mind into this very present moment, NOW! Now has no time, no past or future. Thinking needs time to exist so if you did the above exercise correctly no thoughts would have passed through your mind.

In the absence of thought, it becomes clear: There is only 'this', everything which is appearing in consciousness at this very moment. Differences exist but there is no separation. Everything exists in relationship, within consciousness!

"You are not separate from the whole. You are one with the sun, the earth, the air. You don't have a life, you are life."

Eckhart Tolle(8)

HOW THE EGOIC MIND
CREATES CONFLICT

Humpty Dumpty sat on a wall.
Humpty Dumpty had a great fall.
All the King's horses and all the King's men,
Could not put Humpty together again.

A children's nursery rhyme that sums the situation up:

In the beginning, there was consciousness which was whole, inclusive of everything.
From out of consciousness arose mind.
Mind being discriminatory, separated everything into this and that.
All the clever people tried to use mind to put everything back into wholeness …....and failed miserably!

The flow of individual thoughts we experience is rapid and seemingly unceasing. It builds layer after layer and in doing so gives the illusion of substance.

That apparent solidity confirms ego, our felt, embodied sense of self.

The first point of separation is the single thought, "I am!" or "I exist!". 'I' creates the separation with 'not I'. 'Me' creates the separation with 'not me'. 'Mine' creates the separation with 'not mine'.

Once the ego arises it then establishes itself by constructing an identity:
My family
My house
My street
My community
My friends
My village/town/city/county/region
My religion
My gender
My race
My culture
My history
My country/state
My nationality
My language
My motor vehicle/motorbike/etc.
My sexuality
My wife/husband/partner
My pet/dog/cat/etc.
My children
My job/business
Etc.

With each of those divisions also comes 'not my'. Thought as ego continually divides, fragments and separates the whole of reality. Anything not I, me or mine is someone else's.

To enhance its feeling of security, the ego continues to expand by identifying with other people closest to it in terms of appearance, location and beliefs.

Soon we have 'our house', 'our family', 'our street', 'our country', 'our language', 'our nationality', 'our religion', etc., and 'not our'.

Compounding the problem further still, the ego remains stable and unchanging regardless of any external change. Take the ageing process which, over a seven year period, every cell in a human body is replaced. The ego remains unaffected.

I look in the mirror What do I see?
Bright eyes in a body Looking at me.
That's me I say, Standing young, strong and proud.
So certain am I, I shout it out loud.

But then the years pass,
No longer so bold.
No voice with which to shout,
No certainty to uphold.

I look in the mirror,
Now what do I see?
Dimmed eyes, withered body,
Can that really be me?

Throughout this life,
Change is all.
But no change in my self,
Can I recall.

It's a mystery,
Beyond the mind's eye.
Pray I discover the Truth,
Before I die.

It is obvious when we look, our experiences are always changing but our consciousness never changes. We end up with a subject-object existence in which we are the 'subject' and everything else is an 'object' outside of us.

Now we are in our own personal mental prison with no easy means of escape nor any desire to do so. 'I' loves being 'me'. It has become the most important thing in existence! The consequence of this separative, egoic process is a continuum:

We are always moving away from fears and towards desires, whatever those fears and desires may be. This movement is life as we know it, always away from or toward something.

The core egoic emotion is fear. Ego fears its own non-existence. Consequently, we fear our ending. We fear death. Death is of the body within which thought arises and identifies with. We think we will be annihilated and so fearing this and desiring to live, we keep moving. We dare not stop and look at what is happening and why, nor at who and what we really are.

Ego knows no bounds. As it moves, it produces a process of which we are often unconscious. It pushes us to achieve desires even if in achieving those desires we unwittingly harm other people, other creatures and even the planet. We want to get wealthy, have a beautiful partner, a fantastic house, a top of the range motor vehicle, to travel the world, and in the end to be recognised as 'great' in the eyes of other people.

Once we achieve our goals ego finds new ones to chase in a spiral of never ending desires. Ego can never be satisfied and ultimately results in greed! Being the separative force in human life and the destructive force on our planet, ego, the result of psychological thinking, lies at the core of all human conflict.

If we want conflict to end then we, as we currently exist, have to end. We have to evolve by going beyond our egoic sense of self. This can only be done by each one of us turning inward to discover the truth of who and what we really are.(9)

An insightful description of unconscious egoic desire:

"You want peace. There is no one who does not want peace. Yet there is something else in you that wants the drama, wants the conflict. You may not be able to feel it at this moment. You may have to wait for a situation or even just a thought that triggers a reaction in you; someone accusing you of this or that, not acknowledging you, encroaching on your territory, questioning the way you do things, an argument about money.

Can you then feel the enormous surge of force moving through you, the fear, perhaps being masked by anger or hostility? Can you hear your own voice becoming harsh or shrill, or louder and a few octaves lower? Can you be aware of your mind racing to defend its position, justify, attack, blame?

In other words, can you awaken at that moment of unconsciousness? Can you feel that there is something in you that is at war, something that feels threatened and wants to survive at all cost, that needs the drama in order to assert its identity as the victorious character within that theatrical production? Can you feel there is something in you that would rather be right than at peace?"

Eckhart Tolle(10)

There are few people on this planet at present, and indeed throughout history, who have seen through their mind's conditioning to penetrate the ego. What would a world without ego be like?

"Without ego life would be drama free! Conflict would be replaced with a living sense of ONENESS! All opposition would stop dead in its tracks! Our salvation depends on waking up to the truth: duality is the lie that keeps the dream a grim reality...."

Dr Gregory E. Tucker (11)

'Duality' is our sensed feeling of being separate.

THOUGHT IS THE PROBLEM

"The best way to solve any problem is to remove its cause."

Martin Luthor King Jnr

All of the immense problems we are experiencing today are the result of the action of thought which is dominated by psychological thinking. Every form of conflict beginning with 'me' and 'not me', ultimately ending in war, is the result of the operation of our conditioned minds.

Functional thinking is entirely essential and not a problem, but it is barely noticeable given the prominence of psychological thinking. When academics and commentators discuss the thought process, they are mostly discussing psychological thinking.

We take thought for granted as natural and normal but do not see what it is doing. Thought believes it represents reality accurately but it does not. It abstracts from the whole and so can never be other than an approximation of reality. It has to make assumptions in order to function effectively, with the primary assumption being that 'I' exist in separation from everyone and everything else.

We do not see that it is conditioned by experience and is therefore limited. Its limitation means that thought does something but then fails to recognise that it is responsible for the outcome. Consequently, in seeking to solve problems (and conflicts) it does not realise that it is actually creating complexity, leading to more difficult problems in future

Whilst psychological thought dominates our life we will always be subconsciously on guard, always looking out for potential threats to our ego, always trying to survive and 'get ahead'. We will never have peace in our lives.

"Perhaps, to find the nearest war – and peace – all we need to do is sit home, turn off, tune in and watch the parade in our mind. After all, it's the mind that produces all conflict, that makes war and, when not burdened with belief, rests in peace."

James Waite(12)

IN PURSUIT OF PEACE

"Peace cannot be kept by force; it can only be achieved by understanding."

Albert Einstein

There are two fundamental problems with current forms of conflict resolution methodologies.

1. The Conflict Resolver

The first lies with the conflict resolvers themselves. Taught to be neutral and independent, they still carry with them their own experiences, beliefs, values and attitudes. This subconscious content informs their actions and responses often creating agendas of which they are unaware.

They may have an unshakable faith in their training and methodologies, believing they will be able to resolve all or at least mitigate most of the conflicts they deal with. Even when they think they have resolved a conflict however, the participants who generated it in the first place continue as before. It is only a matter of time before those participants get involved in another conflict situation or the existing one, seemingly resolved, resurfaces.

The insightful conflict resolver has intimate self knowledge. They have dug down into the hidden recesses of their mind to unearth their assumptions, biases, prejudices, beliefs and values. They have seen their own ego in action. In doing so they can recognise their own, other people's and a situations limitations. They understand that unearthing and resolving the underlying personal causes which gave rise to a conflict in the first place, is the only way to finally resolve it.

In attempting to assist in resolving a conflict the primary aim of the conflict resolver is to make themselves redundant. They do this by focusing on the second fundamental problem, which is the way in which the participants in a conflict communicate both with themselves and one another.

2. How We Converse

Talking with each other appropriately enables participants in a conflict to resolve it themselves.

We express ourselves from our own point of view. All points of view are from minds conditioned by personal experience. In a conversation, two participants expressing themselves takes the form of discussion. This is okay until a disagreement arises. Then it becomes a debate. If it is a significant disagreement the conversation becomes heated and turns into argument.

Discussion leading to debate and then argument is the process of conflict escalation.

This process is happening all the time, everywhere. It is the result of separation; the ego, the 'me', pursuing its own survival and self-interest at the expense of everyone (and everything) else. In operation it also continually reinforces that felt sense of being separate.

As a species, we need to evolve beyond this particular form of communication. On our current path, we will continue destroying each other and even the planet's ability to sustain life.

Human created climate change is an increasingly serious issue with worldwide temperatures rising to unprecedented levels. Even the Amazon rainforest is being destroyed at an alarming rate in the name of 'progress' and profit. All of it has the same root cause!

"Humankind has not woven the web of life. We are but one thread within it. Whatever we do to the web we do to ourselves. All things are bound together. All things connect."

Chief Seattle, 1854(13)

CAN WE CHOOSE TO EVOLVE?

"In our world everybody thinks of changing humanity and nobody thinks of changing himself."

Leo Tolstoy

Can we ourselves choose to change our behaviours, end our conflicts with each other and evolve?

We can deliberately evolve only by seeing through the ego and the separation it creates. In seeing that we are not separate entities, that we exist in interdependent relationships with other people, other creatures and the environment we could create a new humanity and thereby a new Earth!

How can we do this? By changing our form of communication with ourselves and then with others. We have to turn inward and question ourselves; question our behaviours, motives, intentions, desires, and the things we fear. We have to question everything we currently take for granted. We have to begin by having a dialogue with ourselves. Dialogue is not discussion, debate or argument. Dialogue is not defending a point of view.

Dialogue is understanding the entire context of a situation.(14)

Without seeing and understanding the entire context of a situation it will continue in one form or another.

In relation to conflicts, we simply cannot work together to resolve them when we are defending ourselves, negotiating with one another, dealing in trade offs or trying to change opinions. We need to enter into participatory rather than oppositional communication. We need to enter into dialogue.

Dialogue allows us to move back from psychological thinking to functional thinking. From here we can think together rather than alone and come up with creative solutions for everyone. We work together rather than work against each other.

In dialogue we look at how we perceive ourselves and others, thereby understanding the nature of the relationship. We come to understand the separation between us and look at how that separation might be reduced or removed. Dialogue provides a 'safe zone' in which we can question our individual and collective (group) thinking.

In normal conversation, attacking someone's beliefs, values, opinions, religion, nationality, etc., is an attack upon them. This does not happen in dialogue. We are simply trying to understand people, not change them. In hearing and understanding other people, we come to own their perspectives and are able to reflect upon how they have come to the positions they take up.

There is just one question that the conflict resolver and the participants in conflict must ask themselves, "Are we capable of dialogue?" If not, then the conflict resolver is stuck with established conflict resolution methodologies and the outcomes will be constrained.

THE ELEMENTS OF DIALOGUE

Dialogue is very simple, not at all complicated. There is no need for clever strategies, no need to try to 'win' in an exchange of views. We do not engage in dialogue because we do not know about it. Our conditioned mind takes our current form of communication for granted and we remain unaware of what we, as psychological thought, are doing. Let us wake up, NOW!

1. A Dialogue with Oneself

A dialogue with oneself is the most important element. It leads to understanding our self and how we might be creating conflicts or be contributing to one. It is a serious activity which can be painful for the one undertaking it, but nevertheless allows for the resolution of that pain.

In exploring our own thinking we are able to detach from our conditioned beliefs, values, attitudes and opinions. Done well, we may eventually come to see the limitations they have imposed upon us.

In preparation for a dialogue to try to end a conflict, the conflict resolver begins by getting every participant to look at themselves and how they have arrived at the situation. What are the attitudes, values and beliefs that have brought them to this point? Why are those attributes so important to them?

This is the beginning of having a dialogue with oneself.

Having inducted a participant into having a dialogue with oneself, the conflict resolver can choose to be with the person self inquiring or leave them to it. It is a judgement call. They should however, point out that it takes at least two (seemingly) separate participants to have a conflict and from the point of view of the self, ego, it is almost always believed that the other participants are at fault.

2. Observation

In dialogue we pay attention and observe ourselves as we think, speak, listen, and to our reactions as we hear what others say. We are finding out about ourselves through the 'mirror' of relationship. We can see if our thoughts, words, reactions and behaviours lead to or heighten conflict or to the resolution of issues. This is a fundamental difference from all existing conflict resolution methodologies. In observing ourselves we see our role in a conflict, if we are contributing to it, maintaining it or helping to resolve it.

3. Listening

Listening is as important as speaking. We rarely if ever truly listen. The voice in our head keeps on commenting, agreeing or disagreeing with what we are listening to. Here, we have to suspend our judgemental mind and pay attention. A metaphor for true listening is a cloudless sky. The clouds represent our thoughts. Only without thoughts passing through our minds can we truly listen. We cannot step into another's mind and see situations as they do so we must listen. People are not listening if they interrupt the one who is speaking.

4. Speaking

We must speak our own truth, express ourselves openly and honestly without fear of rejection or humiliation. Those who listen have to agree to this otherwise dialogue is impossible and they will be stuck in the discussion, debate, argument direction of inevitable conflict. Speaking and listening form one single process.

Our personal perspectives are limited by our conditioned experiences. That limitation means we may be mistaken and we have to be open to this.

Respectful listening and speaking, done well, generates a mutual understanding of a situation. It is only through this that a fundamental resolution of a conflict can be arrived at.

5. Collective Responsibility

Participants in a conflict resolution dialogue are collectively responsible for the outcome. They are responsible for ensuring that:

- participants are understood by everyone involved.
- on the basis of the shared understanding that emerges, all participants are responsible for generating a solution to the conflict which is acceptable to everyone.

Participants in a dialogue, although they might not be aware of it, find themselves thinking together rather than separately. They move back from psychological to functional thinking. This enables the generation of solutions that are acceptable to everyone.

6. Back to A Dialogue with Oneself

Post meeting we return to self inquiry. We look at how the meeting went and how we contributed to it. Did it go well? What more could I or we have done? What impact has the experience had upon me? How do I see the situation now? What would I say or do differently next time? Should we have another dialogue meeting?

We go back to exploring our own thinking. If we do it for long enough it will bring us to silence. It is only in silence that we perceive the ego's phantom existence and our interdependency with everyone and everything else.

"When we face problems or disagreements today, we
have to arrive at solutions through dialogue.
Dialogue is the only appropriate method.
One-sided victory is no longer acceptable.
We must work to resolve conflicts in a spirit
of reconciliation and always keep in mind
the interests of others."

The Dalai Lama(15)

THE CONFLICT RESOLVER'S ROLE

Conflict resolvers begin by talking to each participant in the conflict separately, ensuring that they are allowed to express their point of view; to tell their story. They ensure everyone knows the conflict resolver will be doing the same with every participant involved in the conflict and always in the strictest confidence. There will be no sharing of information with anyone else. There are only four questions that need to be answered in conversation with each participant:

1. What is the cause of this conflict as you see it?

All conflict resolvers know that when different participants in a conflict are asked to determine its cause(s), they usually come up with contrasting answers. Their perceptions are different and this comes down to ego; psychological thought in action.

2. How have you contributed to or are contributing to the conflict?

A question to shock a participant out of the defensive positions they take up. In every conflict it is nearly always perceived to be the other participant's fault and a dogmatic participant will refuse to answer the question. They may even become enraged. When it is pointed out that it always takes two (apparently) separate participants to have a conflict, there has to be a moment of reflection.

3. Do you really want a resolution of this conflict?

Of course everyone wants to resolve their conflicts, yes? No, they don't. Some live for their conflicts. Most want to win! That is what ego always wants. It does not take much 'digging' on the part of the conflict resolver to unearth if a resolution is truly wanted by a particular participant. They do that by asking the final question.

4. What are YOU prepared to do to get a resolution of this conflict?

This fundamental question reveals everything about the participants in a conflict.

Most respond by saying, "What do you mean? It is the other participant's fault and it is them that has to change". This question reveals the degree of separation between the participants.

These four questions unearth hidden agendas and make clear the difficulties that will be faced in attempting to achieve a resolution of the conflict. There should be no time limit set for these initial meetings. If you do not have the time, then do not be a conflict resolver.

At the end of the individual meetings, dialogue as a form of communication, different from discussion, debate or argument, should be introduced and the elements taught in depth.

A simple diagram will aid explanation.

The Conflict Resolution Dialogue Process:

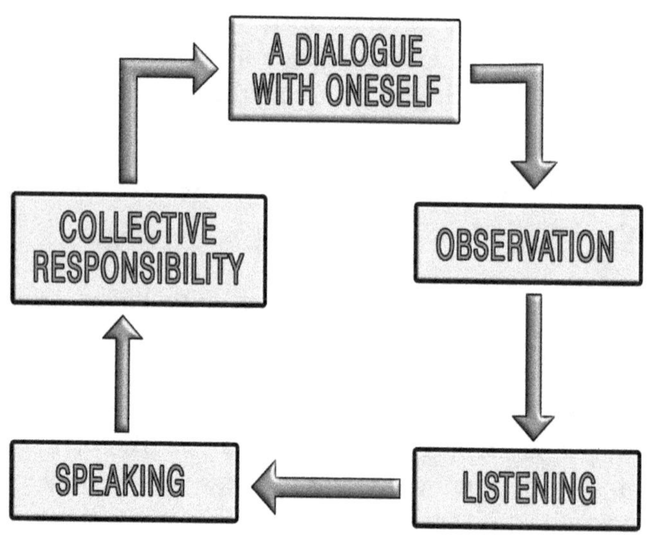

Having listened to every participants story, conflict resolvers are only then in a position to understand the entire context of the situation. They do this by cross referencing all participant answers, to see where there are agreements and differences. The result of this is clarity about the severity of the separation between all the participants involved in the conflict.

Post Individual Participant Meetings

The conflict resolvers are now in a position to assess the conflict and create a suitable resolution approach which fits the entire context of the presenting situation. There are no hard and fast rules, no prescribed methodology to follow. They may decide further individual participant meetings are required before a dialogue takes place.

The conflict resolver must consider if there are any physical, personal, emotional, historical or other barriers that prevent a conflict resolution dialogue taking place? Could these be removed prior to or during a dialogue?

In every case, the point must be made that any areas or subjects not open to inquiry will limit the possibility of conflict resolution and may make it impossible. If the situation is not currently resolvable, then the participants should be informed as to why it is.

Whether the conflict is presently resolvable or not, the re-emphasising of the elements of dialogue in the group context is necessary. This will set the scene for the current or any future conflict resolution meetings that may occur. Should a conflict resolution dialogue be possible, the process may be short or long depending upon the context of the situation. Perhaps it will take several meetings to arrive at a resolution, over days, weeks or months? Perhaps it will take only one meeting?

There has to be a willingness on the part of the participants to continue the dialogue for as long as it takes.

When a dialogue meeting begins the conflict resolver speaks first, facilitating the conversation and always reminding all participants of the elements of dialogue. Each participant in turn is given the opportunity to speak if they wish to do so.

The conflict resolver points out when the dialogue is going 'off course' (people not listening, interrupting, indulging in behaviours that are distracting, etc.). As the meeting progresses they slowly withdraw their input.

A point will be reached when when it is judged that a complete withdrawal is possible and the participants are asked if they would now like to continue without facilitation. If the participants agree, the conflict resolver leaves the meeting. Is that the end of their role?

NO!

They make themselves available should the dialogue meeting participants request their return. Hopefully they will not!

If the participants want the conflict resolver to continue facilitating, then they continue but in as minimal a role as possible. They can judge when the meeting is faltering and suggest ways of moving forward. This might be having a break, side meetings, or agreeing to meet again to allow time for reflection beforehand.

There is no set format or procedures to follow. All decisions and actions are based on the presenting context.

Let the dialogue evolve!

DIALOGUE AIMS TO RESOLVE CONFLICTS BY REDUCING THE DEGREE OF SEPARATION BETWEEN THE PARTIES INVOLVED AND IF POSSIBLE END IT.

IS THERE ANYTHING MORE?

"We build too many walls and not enough bridges."

Isaac Newton

To recount, dialogue is very simple. There is no need for clever strategies or complex procedures.

Ultimately the route to ending all human conflict and evolving beyond it lies in each of us having a dialogue with ourselves and going beyond our ego.

We each think we know ourselves but we do not. How we see the world is entirely a product of our life experiences, which condition our mind to respond in mechanistic ways. Our behaviours become predictable. We become predictable!

"If her past were your past, her pain your pain,
her level of consciousness your level of consciousness,
you would think and act exactly as she does. With this
realization comes forgiveness, compassion and peace."

Eckhart Tolle (16)

The motivation for writing of this short and simple book arose from seeing the immense suffering caused by the war in Ukraine.

It is obvious that neither this war nor any other will lead to an ending of human conflict. There has never been a 'war to end all wars', nor will there ever be as long as the human predicament remains the same. Each and everyone of us, in insisting upon our separate existence, are unwittingly creating conflict all of the time. It really is that simple!

We exist in relationship to everyone and everything else. Psychological thought claims the opposite; that we exist outside of relationship. We do not. We cannot.

Finally, the work you are being left to do yourself: Are you willing to end conflict in yourself? Are you willing to try to evolve beyond egoic consciousness and in doing so contribute to ending all human conflict?

Are you willing to go that far?

"The way of peace is simple. It is the way of truth and love. It starts with the individual himself. Where the individual accepts his responsibility for war and violence, there peace finds a foothold. To go far one must begin near and the first actions are within. The sources of peace are not outside of us and the heart of man is in his own keeping. To have peace, we must be peaceful. To put an end to violence each one must voluntarily free himself from the causes of violence. Diligently one must put himself to the task of self-transformation."

Jiddu Krishnamurti(17)

NOTES

1. This book's content resulted from much research and conducting a substantial number of mediations within urban and rural settings. Applying an initial mediation training's methodology to begin with, the practise evolved through seeing where that methodology succeeded and where it failed. Individual conflicts could seemingly be resolved through 'accommodations' on the part of the participants, however it was noticed that those participants were rarely happy with the outcomes. The methodology used did nothing to change the participants themselves, who then went on to resurrect the conflict or become involved in other ones. It was only when participants were asked to turn back on themselves and look at their role within a conflict that significant progress was made.

2. Conflict resolvers these days are most often referred to as mediators. There are also negotiators, arbitrators and simply, facilitators. Solicitors, lawyers and judges are also types of conflict resolvers. Given the variety of types and the fact that this book is for everyone, regardless of who or what they are, the term 'conflict resolver' is used in the text.

3. Jiddu Krishnamurti, "The First and Last Freedom" (1975).

4. Rupert Spira, YouTube video, "Explaining War".

5. Max Planck, "Where is Science Going" (1932).

6. Adyashanti, "The End of Your World" (2010).

7. This exercise was originated by Steven Harrison, author of "Doing Nothing: Coming to the End of the Spiritual Search", "Being One", and several other books.

8. Twitter post, 29/04/13 (unable to verify).

9. Asking every human being to turn inwards and seek who and what they really are is unrealistic as there are now around 8 billion of us on the planet.

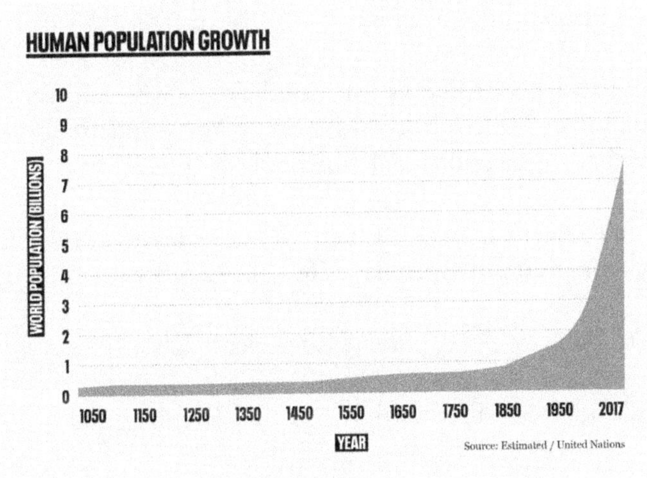

Nearly all live through their ego. It must begin with those who feel able and as many leaders in every country as possible. A 'critical mass' of people need to move beyond egoic consciousness for it to end. Only then would the world as we know it now change. Competition would become cooperation, fighting with one another would be replaced by seeking to help one another, and the planet, with all its species, would be revered. It is a large improbability but not an impossibility!

10. Eckhart Tolle, "A New Earth" (2006).

11. Dr Gregory E. Tucker, Facebook post, 08/07/2022.

12. James Waite, Facebook post, 18/02/2022.

13. Quoted extensively on the Internet but without reference to time or place

14. This is not Plato's form of dialogue which looks for ultimate Truth. It draws heavily on physicist David Bohm's concept of dialogue but is simpler.

15. Dalai Lama, "Open Your Heart: Practicing Compassion in Everyday Life", (2002).

16. Eckhart Tolle, "Stillness Speaks" (2003).

17. Jiddu Krishnamurti, Radio talk (Bombay, 1948).

FURTHER READING

Adyashanti: "The Way of Liberation".

David Bohm: "On Dialogue", "Thought as a System".

Tim Cliss: "This Deafening Silence".

Jeff Foster: "Life Without a Centre".

Steven Harrison: "Doing Nothing: Coming to the End of the Spiritual Search", "Being One". Jiddu

Krishnamurti: "On Conflict", "On Mind and Thought", "Understanding Ourselves".

Rupert Spira: "Being Aware of Being Aware"; "You Are the Happiness You Seek"; "Explaining War" (YouTube video, 2012).

Steve Taylor: "The Fall", "Waking from Sleep", "Back to Sanity".

Eckhart Tolle: "A New Earth", "The Power of Now", "Stillness Speaks".

J C Tefft: videos on YouTube: "Pure Consciousness: The Last Frontier", "The Nature of Mind" Parts 1 and 2, "The End of the Sense of Separateness".

James Waite: "Real, Whole, Here and Happy".

Alan Watts: "The Book on The Taboo Against Knowing Who You Really Are", "The Wisdom of Insecurity", "Ego Death Will Save the World" (YouTube video).

Steven Wolinsky: "Quantum Consciousness".

For the science bit:

David Bohm: "Wholeness and the Implicate Order".

Tom Kitt: "Eternal Recurrence: A Step Out of Time".

Peter Russell: "From Science to Consciousness".

Michael Talbot: "The Holographic Universe".

Jimmy Wu: "Consciousness Revolution" Books 1 and 2.

Traditional Mediation and Conflict Resolution texts:

Jennifer E. Beer & Caroline C. Packard, "The Mediator's Handbook".

Gerry O'Sullivan, "The Mediator's Toolkit".

Gerard Shaw, "7 Winning Conflict Resolution Techniques".

Tony Whatling, "Mediation Skills and Strategies".

www.ingramcontent.com/pod-product-compliance
Lightning Source LLC
Chambersburg PA
CBHW050757240726
48654CB00008B/524